EXPLORING SCIENCE

PHYSICAL CHANGE

RESHAPING MATTER

BY DARLENE R. STILLE

Content Adviser: Paul Ohmann, Ph.D., Assistant Professor of Physics,
University of St. Thomas, St. Paul, Minnesota

Science Adviser: Terrence E. Young Jr., M.Ed., M.L.S.,
Jefferson Parish (Louisiana) Public School System

Reading Adviser: Susan Kesselring, M.A., Literacy Educator,
Rosemount-Apple Valley-Eagan (Minnesota) School District

COMPASS POINT BOOKS · MINNEAPOLIS, MINNESOTA

Compass Point Books • 3109 West 50th Street, #115 • Minneapolis, MN 55410

Visit Compass Point Books on the Internet at www.compasspointbooks.com
or e-mail your request to custserv@compasspointbooks.com

Photographs ©: Greg Probst/Corbis, cover; Erik Leigh Simmons/The Image Bank/Getty Images, 4; Carlos Casariego/The Image Bank/Getty Images, 5; Tom Till/Stone/Getty Images, 6; Chinch Gryniewicz; Ecoscene/Corbis, 8; Tom Stewart/Corbis, 10; H. Prinz/Corbis, 11; Rick Gayle Studio/Corbis, 12; Charles O'Rear/Corbis, 15; Martha McBride/Unicorn Stock Photos, 16; Greg Pease/Stone/Getty Images, 17; OneBlueShoe, 19; Democritus 1692, Coypel, Antoine/Louvre, Paris, France/Bridgeman Art Library, 20; Danny Lehman/Corbis, 21; Jana Birchum/Getty Images, 23; Roy Morsch/Corbis, 24; Jim Shippee/Unicorn Stock Photos, 25; Lester V. Bergman/Corbis, 26; Paul Avis/Taxi/Getty Images, 27; Leonard Lessin/Peter Arnold, Inc., 28, 31; Michael Prince/Corbis, 29; Lester Lefkowitz/The Image Bank/Getty Images, 30; Sergio Pitamitz/Corbis, 33; Paul Almasy/Corbis, 34; M. Dillon/Corbis, 35; NASA/Corbis, 37; John M. Roberts/Corbis, 39; NASA, 40; Corbis, 41; Chris Farina/Corbis, 42; Lori Adamski Peek/Stone/Getty Images, 44; Digital Vision, 46.

Editor: Nadia Higgins
Designer/Page Production: The Design Lab
Lead Designer: Jaime Martens
Photo Researcher: Marcie C. Spence
Illustrator: Farhana Hossain
Educational Consultant: Diane Smolinski

Managing Editor: Catherine Neitge
Creative Director: Keith Griffin
Editorial Director: Carol Jones

Library of Congress Cataloging-in-Publication Data
Stille, Darlene R.
    Physical change : reshaping matter / by Darlene R. Stille.
        p. cm. — (Exploring science)
    Includes bibliographical references and index.
    ISBN 0-7565-1257-3
    1. Matter—Properties—Juvenile literature. I. Title. II. Exploring science (Minneapolis, Minn.)
    QC173.36.S753 2006
    530—dc22   2005002476

About the Author

Darlene R. Stille is a science writer and author of more than 70 books for young people. When she was in high school, she fell in love with science. While attending the University of Illinois, she discovered that she also loved writing. She was fortunate enough to find a career as an editor and writer that allowed her to combine both of her interests. Darlene Stille now lives and writes in Michigan.

TABLE OF CONTENTS

What Is Physical Change?

PHYSICAL CHANGE HAPPENS all around us every day. Outside, an icicle melts in the warmth of the noonday sun. The water trickles down to the icy tip and drips onto the ground.

At home, a pot of soup boils on the stove, sending puffs of steam

into the air. The soup is ladled into bowls. You add salt, and the salt dissolves into the liquid.

In a studio, a sculptor chips away at a block of stone, carving a statue. Builders cut wood for a new house at a construction site. At a factory, copper is stretched into long, thin wires.

Everywhere, objects in our lives are undergoing physical change. Their physical properties—such as shape, temperature, and size—are changing.

Blowing glass is an example of a physical change. Here, heated glass is shaped into a goblet.

MATTER AND HOW IT CHANGES

Icicles, water, stone, and copper are very different things. They all have one thing in common, however. They are all made of matter. Everything in the universe is made of matter, and matter is constantly changing. It changes in two basic ways. One kind of change is called chemical change. Another kind of change is called physical change.

When matter undergoes a chemical change, an entirely new substance is created. Setting fire to wood causes chemical changes. As it burns, the wood changes into wispy smoke and powdery ashes. Smoke and ash are not at all like the original wood. They are made of new chemical substances.

A rusted anchor on a ship has undergone a chemical, as opposed to a physical, change. Rust is a completely new substance unlike the anchor's original metal.

After physical change, the look or feel of matter may be different, but no new substances are made. When a piece of wood is chopped in half, the two smaller pieces are still wood—just with a different shape and size. Mixing and separating are physical changes, too, such as tossing vegetables in a salad or taking apart a puzzle.

But not all physical changes are so obvious. When water freezes into ice or evaporates into steam, the ice and steam may

Water changes easily from a liquid to a solid or a gas—and then back again. For that reason, water is the only substance that can be found in nature in all three states. Other substances can be changed to all three states, but only with human interference.

DID YOU KNOW?

EXPANDING ICE

The volume of the solid state of a substance usually is less than the volume of its liquid state. This means that the solid state of a substance takes up less space than its liquid state. Water is an exception to this rule. Water expands when it freezes, so ice takes up more space than liquid water. Because of this unusual behavior, a sealed glass bottle of water will break if it freezes.

seem like new substances. They are, however, just different states of water. Ice is the solid form of water, and steam is the gaseous form of water. Changing from one state of matter to another is a physical change.

Dissolving is another physical change that may be difficult to recognize. When you stir sugar into a cup of water, the sugar seems to disappear. Drink the water, though, and it tastes sweet. No new substances have been created. The sugar is still there. It has broken down, or dissolved, into microscopic particles.

In general, physical changes are easily reversible, while chemical changes are not. The leftover ash from a fire cannot change back into wood. However, ice easily melts back into water, and steam condenses back into water drops. Mixtures can be separated and mixed back up again. Even dissolved substances can

easily return to their original forms. If a cup of water with sugar dissolved in it is left out, the water will evaporate. The original sugar will be left behind in the bottom of the cup.

Seawater has evaporated from these shallow pans, leaving behind salt that will be collected and used.

CHAPTER TWO

Physical Change and Molecules ⊕

ANOTHER WAY TO TELL the difference between chemical change and physical change is to understand what is happening to atoms during these changes. Atoms are the building blocks of all matter. They are also tiny—much too small to be seen even with an ordinary microscope. Atoms join together to make up slightly bigger units of matter called molecules.

There are many different kinds of atoms, such as carbon atoms or gold atoms. A water molecule is made up of two kinds of atoms—oxygen atoms and hydrogen atoms.

During chemical change, molecules change. When electricity is run through water, water molecules break apart into individual hydrogen and oxygen atoms. The hydrogen atoms join with each other, and new hydrogen molecules made of two atoms are formed. Oxygen atoms also join with each other

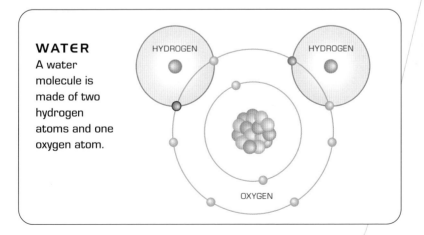

WATER
A water molecule is made of two hydrogen atoms and one oxygen atom.

HYDROGEN

HYDROGEN

OXYGEN

to make oxygen molecules. The hydrogen and oxygen molecules that are produced by this chemical change are no longer water.

During physical change, molecules don't change. They just move closer together or farther apart. For example, as water evaporates into gas, its molecules drift apart. As water vapor condenses into liquid, its molecules move closer together.

MOLECULES AND STATES OF MATTER

What makes a solid a solid? What makes a liquid a liquid and a gas a gas? The answer has to do with how molecules line up and move around.

In solids, the atoms and molecules vibrate, but mostly stay in one place. These slow-moving molecules stick

Solids, such as a lump of clay, have their own shape.
That shape may be molded, though, as it is by this potter.

LIQUID METAL

Nondigital thermometers have a thin line of silvery material, liquid mercury, that shows the temperature. We think of metals as being solid forms of matter, but mercury is a metal that is liquid at room temperature. Mercury freezes into a solid at -38 degrees Fahrenheit (-38.9 degrees Celsius).

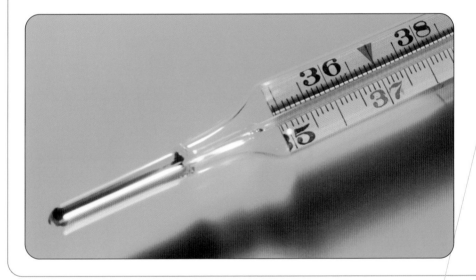

close together. That's why a solid always has its own definite shape. Any solid—such as gold, a sponge, or a grain of sand—can be held in your hand. It doesn't need to be held in a container.

In liquids, molecules are usually farther apart than they are in solids. They slip and slide around each other. That's why liquids spill. They don't have their own shapes. They take the shapes of the containers that hold them.

Gas molecules are not packed together at all. They zip and zoom every which way. For this reason, gases, like liquids,

Here, water takes the shape of the glasses that hold it. However, the liquid levels off. Water doesn't expand to fill the container the way a gas would.

STATES OF MATTER

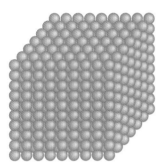

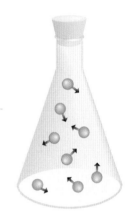

SOLID

Solid objects, such as a block of wood, are made of molecules that are packed closely together. These molecules vibrate. Solids have their own definite shapes.

LIQUID

Liquids like water are made of molecules that are farther apart and move around each other. Liquids take the shapes of their containers.

GAS

Gas molecules, like oxygen, move freely in all directions, usually at high speeds. They expand to completely fill whatever container they are in.

don't have their own shapes. Unlike liquids, however, gases don't level off. They will expand to completely fill whatever container they are in. The same amount of gas can fill a small birthday balloon or a huge metal tank.

"Super" States of Matter

Imagine a liquid so runny that it pours right out through the sides of a cup. Imagine an electric cord plugged into an outlet in New York City and stretched across the United States to operate a vacuum cleaner in San Francisco. Such things could be possible because of special kinds of physical change that create super states of matter.

Solids, liquids, and gases are states of matter found in nature. Some states of matter, however, exist only in the laboratory. Two such states are called superfluids and superconductors. Scientists can change certain liquids into superfluids and some solids into superconductors by special, artificial means.

All liquids have a property called viscosity. The viscosity of a liquid is a kind of resistance in the substance that controls how fast or slow the liquid flows. Molasses has a high viscosity, so it flows very slowly. Water has a low viscosity, so it flows fast.

Superfluids have no viscosity at all. A superfluid can gush right through microscopic holes in a glass or cup. The only substances that scientists have been able to change into superfluids are helium and hydrogen. They did this by removing heat from the helium and hydrogen atoms. Superfluids need temperatures close to -459.67 degrees Fahrenheit (-273.15 C). Called absolute zero, this is the coldest temperature anything could possibly have.

Many engineers are more interested in making solids that are superconductors. Ordinary metal wires in an electric circuit have a property called resistance. They resist the flow of electric current. Resistance causes wires to heat up. It also decreases the amount of electric power the wires can carry. As the distance increases, the power is lost as heat.

Electric current flows through a superconductor without any resistance at all. Scientists have made metals, ceramics, and other materials into superconductors by chilling them to very low temperatures. Superconducting wires could deliver electricity over long distances. Superconductors could also lead to better computers and electric motors.

One of the properites of a superconductor is that it causes magnetic levitation. Magnets "float" around it, as shown here.

CHAPTER THREE

Changing States of Matter

SO WHAT MAKES MOLECULES move closer together or farther apart? Or, put more simply, what causes melting and freezing? What causes evaporation and condensation? The answer is heat. Adding heat makes molecules move faster. Taking heat away makes molecules slow down.

MELTING AND FREEZING

As heat from the sun warms a patch of ice, the molecules in the ice speed up. They bang into each other and bounce farther apart. At temperatures above 32 degrees Fahrenheit (0 C), the molecules move fast enough to change solid ice into liquid water. This temperature is called the melting point of ice.

The opposite change happens when water gets very cold. The molecules slow down and the water freezes, changing into ice. Liquid water freezes into solid ice at 32 degrees Fahrenheit (0 C). This temperature, which is the same as the melting point, is called the freezing point of water. At temperatures

One of ice's properties is that it strongly attaches to the objects it forms upon, like an icicle to a branch. Icicles can be several feet long before they are heavy enough to break and fall to the ground.

above the freezing/melting point, a substance becomes a liquid. At temperatures below the freezing/melting point, a substance becomes a solid.

However, different substances have different melting and freezing points. It takes a lot of heat energy to melt iron, for example. The melting point of iron is 2,795 degrees Fahrenheit (1,535 C). At this temperature, iron turns into a red-hot liquid. Factories melt iron to make many things. Liquid iron can be poured into molds. When the iron cools back to a solid, it may have the shape of a patio chair or a frying pan.

Molten, or melted, steel will be poured into molds and cooled quickly by cold water. As it cools, it will harden into desired shapes.

RED-HOT ENGINES

The main structure of a car engine begins as red-hot liquid metal. Workers pour the liquid metal into a mold shaped like an engine. When the liquid metal cools, it changes into a solid auto engine block.

BOILING AND CONDENSING

Water heats in a teakettle on the stove. When the water gets hot enough, steam comes out of the spout, and the teakettle starts to whistle. What happened?

Adding heat energy to the molecules of liquid makes the molecules fly around faster and faster. They fly farther and farther apart. When the molecules are moving fast enough, the liquid evaporates into a gas. This happens most quickly when a liquid boils. The boiling point of water is 212 degrees Fahrenheit (100 C).

The steam from the teakettle falls on a cool windowpane above the stove. The gas cools below 212 degrees Fahrenheit (100 C) and changes back into drops of liquid water that run down the glass. Cooling makes molecules move slower and get closer together. When the molecules slow down enough, the gas condenses, or changes into a liquid.

Boiling and condensation points are different for different substances. Iron boils at 5,432 degrees Fahrenheit (3,000 C). The

condensation point of oxygen gas is -297 degrees Fahrenheit (-183 C). Below this temperature, oxygen gas changes to a pale, blue liquid.

Invisible water vapor in the air has condensed into droplets of dew on leaves. Dew is most common on humid mornings when the temperature is above freezing.

The Study of Matter

The idea of how matter changes from solid to liquid to gas came from the work of many scientists over thousands of years. Each scientist built on the ideas of others. In the 400s B.C., two ancient Greeks, Leucippus and Democritus, developed the idea that everything is made of atoms. Democritus also believed that atoms move and collide with each other.

Scientists did not know that there were three ordinary states of matter until the 1600s. Before this, they knew about solids and liquids. Then they began to suspect that there was a state of matter like air. A Belgian chemist named Jan Baptista van Helmont called this form of matter "gas." The name comes from a Greek word meaning "space."

Scientists then learned that many substances can change from one state of matter to another. They knew that water could go from solid to liquid to gas. But English physicist Michael Faraday, in 1823, was the first person to change another gas into a liquid. He changed chlorine gas into a liquid under pressure in a test tube. Faraday found that he could turn many other gases into liquids.

Scientists in the 1800s also developed the kinetic theory, which explains how molecules move in solids, liquids, and gases.

The Greek philosopher Democritus (460?–370? B.C.) said that atoms, or invisible particles of matter, combined to make up everything in the world. His ideas about atoms proved to be true in great part but were not widely accepted for more than 2,000 years.

Scottish mathematician and physicist James Clerk Maxwell made a major contribution to the kinetic theory of gases. He created a mathematical law that shows how the movement of molecules determines the pressure and temperature of a gas. This study of physical change is a part of physics called thermodynamics. Thermodynamics is about how energy flows.

In the 1900s, physicists began to learn about other states of matter and how physical changes in these states occur. They built gigantic atom-smashing machines called particle accelerators. Subatomic particles whiz through these accelerators and reach the high temperatures and pressures that scientists believe existed soon after the birth of the universe. With the use of high technology, scientists have learned about other states of matter that are not usually seen. Who knows what discoveries are still to be made?

In a particle accelerator, streams of subatomic particles (particles smaller than atoms, such as electrons and protons) travel at incredibly high speeds through airless pipes.

THE ROLE OF PRESSURE

It takes longer to boil an egg in Denver than in Chicago. Why? Because Denver is located at a higher altitude than Chicago.

People often say that the boiling point of water is 212 degrees Fahrenheit (100 C), but that is water's boiling point at sea level. Sea level is the point on Earth that is level with the surface of the ocean. The air pressure at sea level is called normal atmospheric pressure.

Atmospheric pressure describes the force of the gases in air pressing down on the surface of Earth. The lower the surface, the more gas lies above it, and the greater the pressure of the atmosphere.

Atmospheric pressure affects the temperature at which liquid water boils and changes to a gas. The greater the pressure, the more heat it takes for a liquid to boil. Chicago is near sea level, but Denver is 1 mile (1.6 kilometers) above sea level. The atmospheric pressure is greater in Chicago than Denver, so water boils at a higher temperature in Chicago than Denver. It may take longer for water to reach its boiling point in Chicago than it does in Denver, but the boiling water in Chicago is hotter. Food cooks faster in hotter water. All in all, it takes someone in Chicago less time to make a hard-boiled egg than it does in Denver.

Pressure cookers also work on this principle. Sealed pressure cookers hold in the steam created when water boils. The steam creates high pressure. The high pressure creates the high temperatures that allow foods to cook faster than in open pans.

Pressure can also play a role in turning gases to liquids. Many barbecue grills use a gas called propane. The propane is a liquid because it was "stuffed" into a tank. Pushing gas molecules closer together without cooling them increases gas pressure. If the gas molecules are pushed close enough together, their motion will slow and the gas will turn into a liquid. A small tank keeps the propane under high pressure. Turning on the grill opens a valve in the tank, and the gas molecules shoot out. The gas hits a spark and starts to burn.

Liquefied propane gas can be used to fuel trucks. A propane fueling station looks similar to a familiar gasoline one.

DID YOU KNOW?

HOT TIRES

Pumping air into a bicycle tire increases the pressure. The greater the pressure, the harder a tire feels. The pressure is caused by air molecules banging into the inside tire wall. On a hot day, this same amount of air will have a higher pressure than on a cold day. Higher temperatures increase the motion of the air molecules, and this increases the pressure.

SUBLIMATION

Sometimes a solid changes to a gas without first becoming a liquid, or a gas changes directly to a solid. When the liquid state of matter is skipped, the change is called sublimation.

Dry ice is a substance that sublimes. This very cold solid is made of frozen carbon dioxide gas. You can see dry ice sublime. As the vapor rises off the block of dry ice and into the air, the solid is changing directly to a gas. Food companies and drug companies sometimes use dry ice to keep products cold during shipping.

Sublimation is at work in a freezer when a hamburger patty dries out from freezer burn. Sublimation is also at work when patches of snow and ice disappear from the sidewalk on cold winter days. This happens more quickly when the atmospheric pressure is low.

Dry ice gets its name from the fact that it is never wet. It sublimes, or goes from a solid to a gas, without becoming a liquid.

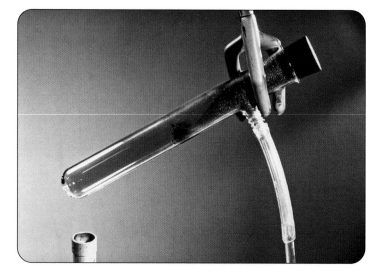

Food companies use sublimation to create freeze-dried foods, such as coffee, soups, fruits, and mushrooms. Freeze-drying does not change the color or texture of the food, something that does happen when food is set out to dry by evaporation. Freeze-dried foods can be kept for years without spoiling. Microorganisms that cause food to spoil need water in order to survive.

The first step in freeze-drying is to freeze all the water in the food. Then the frozen food is placed in a vacuum chamber, a space from which almost all the air has been removed. Removing the air lowers the atmospheric pressure inside the chamber. The frozen food is heated to just below the melting point of water. Because of the lowered pressure, the ice in the food sublimes, or changes to gas.

Sometimes substances sublime by going directly from a gas to a solid. Here, iodine gas (at the bottom of the tube) becomes an iodine solid (the dark purple substance at the top).

Mixing and Separating ⊕

A HANDFUL OF TRAIL MIX shows peanuts, raisins, chocolate chips, and perhaps some cashews. Trail mix is a mixture. Since its components are not chemically combined, they can be separated without a problem. You can easily pick out your favorite pieces.

Trail mix is a mixture of solids, but a mixture can be any combination of solids, liquids, and gases. Foam is a gas mixed with a liquid, for example, and smoke is a solid in a gas (air). Thick fog over an ocean pier is a liquid (tiny drops of water) in a gas (air), while milk is a mixture of two liquids.

One characteristic of mixtures, such as sand and shells, is that they don't follow one fixed "recipe." The proportions of components, or "ingredients," can change.

DIFFUSION

Mixtures can be created by a number of forces, such as stirring or shaking. Some mixtures, called diffusions, happen without the aid of an outside force. They are caused by the natural, random movement of atoms and molecules inside a substance. As steam escapes from a boiling pot, it seems to disappear into the

air. In reality, steam molecules diffuse, or scatter, through the air. Soon, the steam molecules mix in so thoroughly with air molecules that the steam is no longer visible.

If you pour some orange juice into water and let it sit, eventually the mixture will turn completely orange. Like steam in air, the orange juice will diffuse throughout the water, powered by the natural slipping and sliding movements of molecules in liquids.

Vegetable dye diffuses through a glass of water. Eventually, the liquid will turn a uniform blue.

WHAT'S THAT SMELL?

Diffusion explains why smells carry through the air. Tiny molecules from perfume, hot coffee, or other objects shoot through the air. As they diffuse with air molecules, they produce odors that we can smell. Air currents also help spread these odors more quickly.

SUSPENSIONS

Some mixtures, such as trail mix or smoke in the air, are easy to recognize as mixtures. Sometimes the different components can still be seen. Another clue that something is a mixture is if its overall appearance is cloudy, patchy, or full of lumps. These mixtures are called suspensions. Italian salad dressing is a suspension because the oil will separate on its own after just a few minutes of sitting. Because the oil is lighter than vinegar, it rises, forming a distinct layer on the top of the mixture.

A filter is a common way of separating components of a suspension. A filter can be as simple as a fine screen, such

as a filter in a dryer that separates lint from air. Paper filters let
coffee drip through while keeping the grounds out. One common step in cleaning city water is to run it through a filter of
sand on top of gravel. As the water trickles through the thick

Concrete is a suspension of water and sand, gravel, or crushed stone.

layer of sand and gravel, dirt particles are screened out. Some types of engines even use magnets to remove impurities from fuel. Tiny metal particles are attracted to the magnetic filters.

Cream is separated from milk in a machine called a centrifuge. A centrifuge is a wheel-shaped instrument that spins liquid mixtures around at incredibly high speeds. This motion causes heavier components in the mixture to settle to the bottom. The lighter components, such as cream in milk, are left on top.

A centrifuge is also commonly used to separate blood. Blood is a suspension of various types of cells and plasma, the watery liquid that carries the cells around the body. In a centrifuge, blood cells fall to the bottom and the plasma rises to the top. In this way, blood is prepared for its many medical uses.

A lab technician examines a vial of blood that has been spun through a centrifuge. The blood has been separated into layers.

SOLUTIONS

Stir a spoonful of salt into a cup of warm water, and the two will form a solution. The salt will completely dissolve in the water. As it dissolves, the salt breaks down into its smallest units—charged atoms called ions—that spread evenly throughout the water. Because the ions are much too small to see, the salt water looks perfectly clear. The water tastes salty, however, proving that the salt is still present in the mixture. It has not been chemically changed into a new substance.

Solutions can be solids, liquids, or gases, but liquid solutions are more common. Salt water is a solid dissolved in a liquid. A liquid can dissolve in a liquid, too, such as alcohol and water. Bubbly soda is a common solution of gas (carbon dioxide) dissolved in flavored water. One common solid solution—sterling silver—is found inside most jewelry boxes. Sterling silver is a mixture of silver and copper.

Not all substances will form solutions with each other, and those that do have their limits. Sugar will dissolve in iced tea. However, if enough sugar is stirred into a cup of iced tea, grains will appear in the bottom of the cup. The cold tea can only dissolve a certain amount of sugar, so some sugar is left whole. However, raising the temperature will help the process along. Hot tea can dissolve more sugar than an equal amount of iced tea.

Unlike suspensions, solutions cannot be separated by filters or centrifuge. One age-old method of separating a solution is a process called distillation. More than 2,000 years ago, soldiers of ancient Rome used distillation to turn salt water into fresh water suitable for drinking. They removed the salt from seawater through a process called solar distillation.

By today's standards, solar distillation is slow and inefficient, and is not commonly used. However, modern distillation methods are similar to the age-old process. Shallow basins filled with water are placed in the sun. The basins are covered with a see-through plastic dome or an angled sheet of glass. As the sun heats the seawater, the water evaporates, but the salt remains in the bins. When the rising water vapor hits the underside of the plastic or glass cover, it cools and condenses back into water. This water—now pure and without salt—runs down the sloping cover and is collected.

Because it is a solution, salty sea water is just as clear as pure water.

Though modern seawater distillation methods vary, they all rely on evaporating the water and then collecting the condensed water vapor. Distillation is still used on most ships to supply fresh drinking water out at sea.

A homemade water still converts seawater to drinking water through solar energy. The pure water is collected in a glass jar beneath the sloped panel.

Distillation and Petroleum

Another major use of distillation is to separate crude oil, or petroleum. Petroleum is the source of gasoline and many other kinds of fuels that provide much of the world's energy. In its raw form, however, the thick, greenish liquid is an unusable mixture of several kinds of fuel oils, dissolved gases, and impurities. To separate its components, petroleum is processed at an oil refinery.

The distillation process relies on the fact that each component in the crude oil has a different condensing point. For example, gasoline vapor turns to liquid at about 90 degrees Fahrenheit (32 C), while other fuels' condensing points may be more than 600 degrees Fahrenheit (315.5 C).

An oil refinery in Texas City, Texas, is a maze of towers, tanks, pipes, and pumps. Petroleum is a key industry of the state.

HOW CRUDE OIL IS REFINED

Crude oil, or petroleum, is processed at oil refineries to separate its various components, such as fuel oil and gasoline.

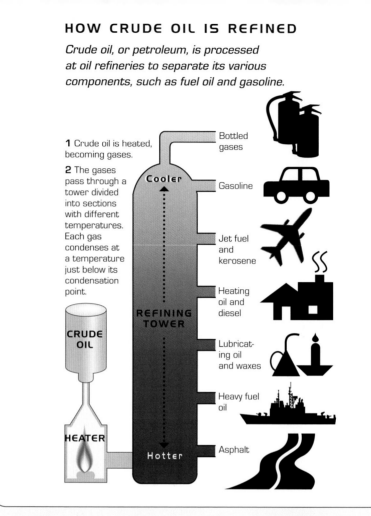

1 Crude oil is heated, becoming gases.

2 The gases pass through a tower divided into sections with different temperatures. Each gas condenses at a temperature just below its condensation point.

Cooler

REFINING TOWER

CRUDE OIL

HEATER

Hotter

Bottled gases

Gasoline

Jet fuel and kerosene

Heating oil and diesel

Lubricating oil and waxes

Heavy fuel oil

Asphalt

The crude oil is heated to more than 650 degrees Fahrenheit (343 C), and the gases rise inside a tall, steel tower. The tower is divided into sections with different temperatures. The sections at the bottom are the hottest, and they gradually become cooler as they rise. As the gases pass through the tower, each one condenses in the section of the tower where the temperature is just below its condensation point. The various condensed liquids are then collected.

Physical Change in Nature ⊕

THE WATER CYCLE

Physical changes are important to Earth's environment. For example, physical changes drive Earth's water cycle. The water cycle is the constant movement of all the water on Earth. Heat from the sun makes water in lakes, rivers, and oceans evaporate. The water changes into water vapor and rises into the air, or atmosphere. When the air is cool enough, the water vapor turns to droplets of liquid water or tiny crystals of ice. The water or ice forms clouds. Finally, the water from the clouds returns to Earth as rain or snow. The water finds its way back to rivers, lakes, and the ocean. The water cycle begins all over again.

This view from outer space shows storm clouds drifting over an ocean. Earth's water is constantly moving and changing states. Because of this, the amount of water on Earth has been the same at least since the beginning of human history.

THE WATER CYCLE

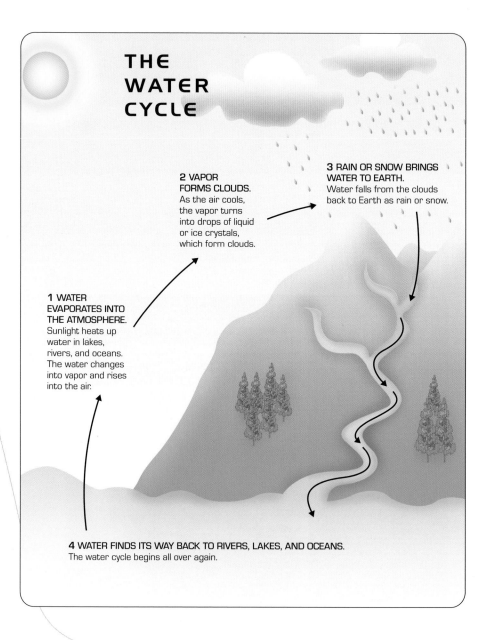

2 VAPOR FORMS CLOUDS.
As the air cools, the vapor turns into drops of liquid or ice crystals, which form clouds.

3 RAIN OR SNOW BRINGS WATER TO EARTH.
Water falls from the clouds back to Earth as rain or snow.

1 WATER EVAPORATES INTO THE ATMOSPHERE.
Sunlight heats up water in lakes, rivers, and oceans. The water changes into vapor and rises into the air.

4 WATER FINDS ITS WAY BACK TO RIVERS, LAKES, AND OCEANS.
The water cycle begins all over again.

WEATHERING

Physical changes in nature also help turn solid rocks into soil. First, liquid water seeps down into tiny cracks in rocks. When it gets cold enough, the water freezes into ice. The solid ice expands, or pushes outward, and breaks the rock apart. Rain and wind then wear down the smaller pieces of rocks. This wearing down of rock is called weathering. It takes thousands of years for rock to be worn down into soil.

Weathering has carved a graceful arch from sandstone at Arches National Park, Utah.

SHINING STARS

What are the sun and stars made of? The answer is not a solid, liquid, or a gas. The sun and stars are made of a special form of matter called plasma.

Physicists call plasma the fourth state of matter. Plasma is a kind of electrified gas. The transformation from gas to plasma is a physical change.

Plasmas contain a special kind of atom that does not have all of its parts. Atoms are very tiny units of matter, much too small to see. But small as they are, each atom is made up of even smaller parts. The center part of an atom is called the nucleus. Even tinier parts called electrons orbit around the nucleus of an atom.

The atoms that make up a plasma have lost some or all of their electrons. Electrons can be stripped away by one of two things—high temperatures or electricity. Stripping electrons away from atoms causes a substance to change its state from a gas to a plasma.

About 99 percent of the universe that astronomers can see is made of plasma.

ATOMS

Atoms are the basic building blocks of all things.

The **nucleus,** or center, of an atom is made up of two types of particles:

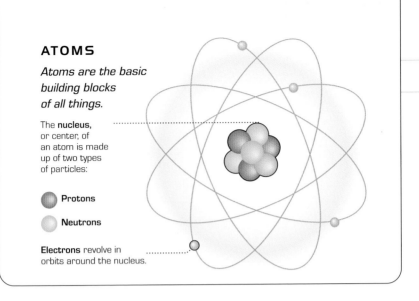

Protons

Neutrons

Electrons revolve in orbits around the nucleus.

The sun and all the other stars are incredibly hot. It is this heat that causes plasma to form. Heat strips electrons away from atoms in the sun. The temperature at the center of our sun reaches 27 million degrees Fahrenheit (15 million C). At these temperatures, nuclear fusion reactions occur in the plasma. In nuclear fusion, the nuclei of two atoms fuse, or join together, and give off huge amounts of energy. The sun's energy comes from these reactions.

DID YOU KNOW?

LIGHTNING PLASMA

You can see lightning strike when gas molecules in air change to a plasma. A huge electric spark flashes between two clouds or between a cloud and the ground. Energy in this powerful spark strips electrons from atoms in the air, making a glowing plasma that you see as a bolt of lightning.

Plasma on Earth

The sun shines brightly on a summer day. A neon sign gives off a colorful glow in a store window at night. It might be hard to imagine that the sun in the sky and a sign in a store window have anything in common, but they do. Like the sun, the neon sign is made from plasma.

102" The Largest TV in the World

Unlike the sun, a neon sign is fairly cool. Instead of heat, an electric current forms the plasma in a neon sign. The current knocks electrons away from atoms of neon gas sealed in a glass tube. The plasma gives off light, and the tube glows.

Plasmas could be one of our main energy sources in the future. Scientists want to use nuclear fusion reactions in plasmas as a safe form of nuclear energy.

To do so, plasmas must be heated to at least 90 million degrees Fahrenheit (50 million C). At these temperatures, the nuclei move fast enough to crash into each other and fuse, or join. This nuclear fusion releases enormous amounts of energy.

One problem is that no container on Earth can hold plasma that is this hot. So physicists are researching the use of magnetic "bottles." Powerful magnetic fields would hold the hot plasma in place.

The thin plasma television sets contain tiny colored fluorescent lights that combine to create the TV picture. The lights work in basically the same way as neon signs. Electric current strips electrons away from atoms in fluorine gas—creating plasma.

GLOBAL WARMING

Many scientists worry that humans are causing physical change that could be harmful to the planet. Since the beginning of the Industrial Revolution in the 1700s, people have been burning increasing amounts of coal, oil, and other fossil fuels. Burning fossil fuels sends a gas called carbon dioxide into Earth's atmosphere.

Carbon dioxide is called a greenhouse gas. Like the glass walls and roofs of a greenhouse, carbon dioxide traps heat energy from the sun. Scientists fear that the trapped heat energy is causing Earth's climate to grow warmer. This process is called the greenhouse effect. Earth's average temperature from all four

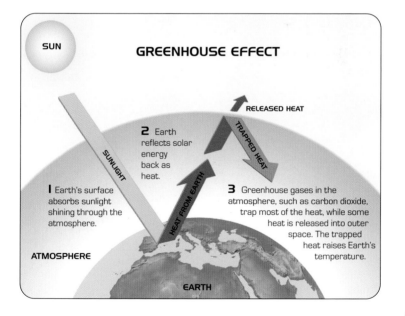

GREENHOUSE EFFECT

SUN

RELEASED HEAT

SUNLIGHT

2 Earth reflects solar energy back as heat.

HEAT FROM EARTH

TRAPPED HEAT

1 Earth's surface absorbs sunlight shining through the atmosphere.

3 Greenhouse gases in the atmosphere, such as carbon dioxide, trap most of the heat, while some heat is released into outer space. The trapped heat raises Earth's temperature.

ATMOSPHERE

EARTH

seasons and from varying climates has risen almost 1 degree Fahrenheit (0.5 C) since 1980. This global increase in heat energy is causing the ice caps at the North and South poles to melt and change into liquid water. Adding more liquid water to the ocean could lead to flooding along coastlines all over the world.

All around us, the processes of physical change—cutting, grinding, molding, melting, freezing, boiling, mixing, and separating—are reshaping matter. Molecules are speeding up and slowing down, moving closer together and farther apart. By shaping matter, physical change shapes the most familiar objects of our world. A quick look around the house, school, yard, and street shows the hundreds of physical changes we encounter and create in our everyday lives.

Even something as simple as riding a bike through a puddle mixes dirt, water, and mud, creating a physical change.

atoms—basic units of matter that are much too small to see; atoms join to make molecules

condensation—the process of turning from a gas to a liquid, usually because of cooling

diffusion—a mixing together of different substances caused by the random motion of molecules and atoms

dissolve—to break down into microscopic units when mixed with another substance

electrons—tiny particles that orbit, or go around, an atom's nucleus

evaporation—the process of turning from a liquid to a vapor, or gas, usually because of heating

filter—a device used to separate a mixture; the mixture is run through a material that allows some substances to pass through while keeping others out

fossil fuels—fuels, including coal, oil, or natural gas, made from the remains of ancient organisms

freeze-drying—a way of preserving food by removing water from it through sublimation (having water change directly from ice to vapor)

molecule—a building block of matter made up of two or more atoms

nuclear fusion—atomic nuclei combining to form a larger nucleus, usually releasing energy

nuclei—the center parts of atoms; *nuclei* is the plural of *nucleus*

plasma—an electrified gas; often called the fourth state of matter

properties—qualities in a material, such as color, hardness, or shape

solutions—uniform mixtures obtained by dissolving one substance into another

sublimation—the direct change in state from a solid to a gas or a gas to a solid

suspensions—mixtures in which one substance has not been dissolved in the other

viscosity—a property of a liquid that has to do with how fast it flows

volume—the amount of space taken up by a substance

▶ Substances change into another strange state at temperatures that are close to absolute zero, the coldest temperature matter can achieve. When atoms are this cold, they slow down until they are almost not moving at all. Millions of atoms may then start to behave as though they are one big atom. This cold state of matter is called a Bose-Einstein condensate. It was named for the two scientists who theorized in the 1920s that this state of matter exists—Indian physicist Satyendra Nath Bose and German-born American physicist Albert Einstein.

▶ Freezing seawater is another way to remove salt from it. Frozen seawater, such as icebergs, contains almost no salt at all.

▶ Why do people sprinkle salt on their icy sidewalks? Salt lowers ice's freezing point. The ice will melt faster, saving on scraping and shoveling. Also, salt raises water's boiling point. Add salt to a bubbling pot of water and the water will settle down almost immediately, at least for a short while.

▶ You can feel the energy of motion in atoms and molecules. You feel this energy as temperature. Molecules in ice have less energy of motion than do molecules in water. For this reason, you feel ice as being cold.

▶ One use for superconductors is in making electromagnets for maglev trains. These powerful magnets lift the train above the tracks and let it speed along on a cushion of air. A prototype maglev train, powered by low-temperature super-conducting electromagnets, was tested in Japan in 1999 and reached a top speed of 342 miles (547 km) per hour— a world record.

▶ Plasma might be important in future space exploration. For example, powerful plasma fuel might power rocket ships that carry astronauts farther than they ever have before—perhaps to the outer edges of the solar system or even to other stars.

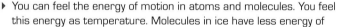
Almost all substances can become liquids at the right temperature—even rock. Lava is melted rock that shoots out of volcanoes from inside Earth.

At the Library

Baldwin, Carol. *States of Matter.* Chicago: Raintree, 2004.
Ballard, Carol. *Solids, Liquids, and Gases: From Ice Cubes to Bubbles.* Chicago: Heinemann Library, 2004.
Cooper, Christopher. *Matter.* New York: DK Children, 1999.
Hunter, Rebecca. *The Facts About Solids, Liquids, and Gases.* North Mankato, Minn.: Smart Apple Media, 2005.
Tocci, Salvatore. *Experiments with Heat.* New York: Children's Press, 2002.

On the Web

For more information on **physical change**, use FactHound to track down Web sites related to this book.
1. Go to *www.facthound.com*
2. Type in a search word related to this book or this book ID: **0756512573**
3. Click on the *Fetch It* button.
FactHound will find the best Web sites for you.

On the Road

Space Science Institute
4750 Walnut St., Suite 205
Boulder, CO 80301
720/974-5888
www.spacescience.org
To visit the Electric Space Exhibit and learn more about plasma in the universe

Alabama Iron & Steel Museum
Tannehill Ironworks Historical State Park
12632 Confederate Parkway
McCalla, AL 35111
205/477-5711
www.tannehill.org/museum.html
To see exhibits of Civil War blast furnaces for melting iron

Explore all the books in this series

Chemical Change
From Fireworks to Rust

Erosion
How Land Forms, How It Changes

Manipulating Light
Reflection, Refraction, and Absorption

Minerals
From Apatite to Zinc

Natural Resources
Using and Protecting Earth's Supplies

Physical Change
Reshaping Matter

Soil
Digging Into Earth's Vital Resource

Waves
Energy on the Move